WINTER,
GLOSSOLALIA

T0018677

John James Winter,
Glossolalia

THE **BLACK SPRING**
PRESS GROUP

First published in 2022
by Eyewear Publishing Ltd.,
an imprint of Black Spring Publishing Group
United Kingdom

Typeset with graphic design by Edwin Smet
Author photo by Caleb Perry
All rights reserved © 2022 John James

The right of John James to be identified as author of this work has been asserted in
accordance with section 77 of the Copyright, Designs and Patents Act 1988

ISBN 978-1-915406-23-1

BLACKSPRINGPRESSGROUP.COM

dedicated to
Frederick Smock
in memoriam

TABLE OF CONTENTS

being
riddles itself
into itself

—Ernst Meister, *In Time's Rift*

SMALL VERSION OF A LONG STORY

Impalpable, transparent, a big man
In a rabbit coat turns twice, turns three times
Toward the sun. And then away.

Reveals the storied longing he totes.
The yellow pain that he's been gifted.

From winter to rank spring
He descends snowy mountains,
Lewd, and plucking bluemonk from the vine.

Fig. 1 **The Provinces**

GLOSSOLALIA

i.

      Fog clots the air, almost
absent, nasturtiums denuded
              in the small distance.

      Dew pallor gathers
in the park. Ravens
              interrupt. Scraps

      of paper, plastic bags,
the movement of anything
              acknowledging

      the wind's receipt.

ii.

      Ravaged
cabbages, the shell
              of a salted snail

      tossed among dandelion heads, the heads
pricking through
              a brick wall. Fog

      sieves the sound
of a dumptruck
              extracting discarded

matter from a can. White moths
circle a pistil, tongue
                an orchid's yellow fuzz.

iii.

        Crushed glass kneads
the ankle's thrust,
                blood erupts

        on the pavement. Last night's
rain's inscribed
                on a patch of winded

        cellophane wrapped around
a metal hasp.
                Weather's edge,

        your mouth's an open
wound. Clouds
                surround the puncture's

        bright bloom.

TOWARD

Two epigrams

1.

A poplar stump
stammers through the thaw.

Moisture   locked
before
in ice

departs
the frozen ground.

Orchard under
foliage cover

roots   crack
the broken
crust.

2.

Fallen limbs   bundle
in a pit—

flames release
their form.

Carbon lodges   in arboretum
in air—

vultures orbiting
a spit.

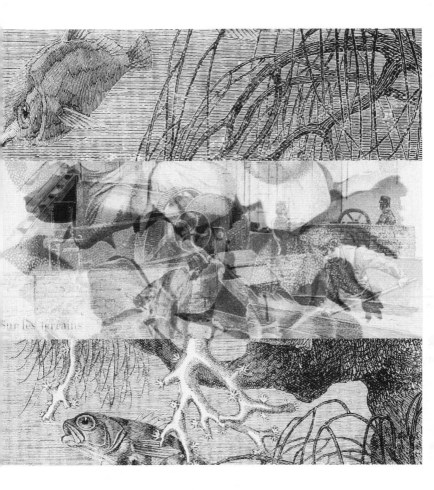

Fig. 2 **Sur Les Terrains**

GRADIENT

dusk sucks pigment
from a canvas of land

gulls go with it

drag west
its planetary turn

·

the day dissolves but you
knew that already

frost accrues

precipitates   a storm

a radiator's dull roll
eclipses wind's hum

temperature degrades

snow hails   thick mist
blotting visibility

       •

detached icicles
strewn

sidelong
about the bank

pavement interjects

hastens frozen
matter's

slow swerve

birch branch   mitigated
you'd say

broken
by the breeze

culled
in the storm's

effacing thrust

·

attenuating
from the eaves

ice divides   my sight

lingers
in the porch's

raucous light

FIG. 402.

Fig. 3 **Fig. 402**

WINTERING

egrets   beached
on a cold day

the color of their wings
almost   absent

the color of the ocean
winding in

abandonment's barb   you stand
on the coast

aluminum scraps
sifting in foam

noon moon
dejects the tide

water levels
rise

flotsam   in place

a buoy
floats the rope

sight inscribes a thought
on the seascape's
tome

tan grass
in thin wind

smudges the   untouched
sky

gust of gulls

        the motor slurs

mussels grip
the post

water   licks
the jetty
clean

it washes
it lashes

bolted together
freely tarred,

Fig. 4 **Bolted | Tarred**

SCALABILITY

Arches inarticulate in the sun's swell.

Silence feasts on birds.

Blotted by its own light, the moon accrues its bloom.

It tugs the sea's lip.

These bricks have a thousand

      Thousand years. My hands

Are in their twenties.

Words won't say what's beyond the page, won't gather

      Thought into a print.

The gaudy script of a neon sign

Bars the night's heat.

THRUST

The purple-stippled,
brindled cultivars defeat
the heat, wrest moisture
from topsoil desiccated
by the sun's dialectic
with the earth, ripe plums
further ripened, the fogged light
chalked across their skin
gesturing to the red flesh:
the plant supplants a word, world.

Fig. 5 **Mutability**

MOUNTAIN SONG

i. Slight

Dull sickle in the shed,
wasp swallowed
in a pod. The fig
in your hand
is obscene.

Red. You called the mums
phosphor red, tongue eclipsed
in a cluster of Os.

Morning enters.
The rose
revises its stem.

Flowers exchange
with the bee.

ii. *To a Mosquito*

The rosy blotch of him
smeared across my wrist
is a blood moon in September.
None of this can last, it's true.

I pluck a grape from the stem,
crush the ripe flesh on the roof
of my mouth, swish its seed
along the grid of my teeth.

The blood on my arm,
freckles on your wrist.
Birds shuffle and depart.

iii. *Surface Speak*

Grammar's torque
wound around
a wound.

Thought's as real as stone.
Ragweed, orchard green,
mounds of damaged apples.
An aspen leaf's
brief shape.

Material drifts, a raven
needling the sky.

Tomato flowers,
cigarette butts,
whatever water
you want.

iv. *Garden Time*

Clipped stems
in their unutterable nakedness.
Seeds in the dirt, a pair
of worked gloves.
Where thinking
goes when you die.
I am not my body,
not root
nor rhizome.
You place your hand
on my wrist.
I branch out
in the earth's breath,
tunnels carved
by worms.

v. *After Neruda / After Tranströmer*

Rain hammers a tin roof.
You tip your nose to the sky.
The fish in the salt of the sea shut their eyes.

The surface of the lake
whispers down through the surface of lilies.
I wish them dead then I don't.

Thunder rumbles.
The closed country answers.
A roar of mingled notes.

vi. *White Mountains*

We sleep through years in a sleeping house,
ghosts alight in the field.
I stand on a mountain
behind sidewalk cafés,
watch boats
clash in the harbor.

vii. *After Rilke / After Bly*

As children we planted forests,
dropped their roots in the mud
and watched their canopies unfold.
Earth has pulled so many nights down.

Our sadness is being saddled now.
The sun brushes the lip of the sea.
Grief is the only bread I eat,
such as is stored in the amygdala.

An old horse stands in the rain.
We lift each other onto its back.
Come with me, if only for a moment.
Heavy are the mountains, heavy the seas.

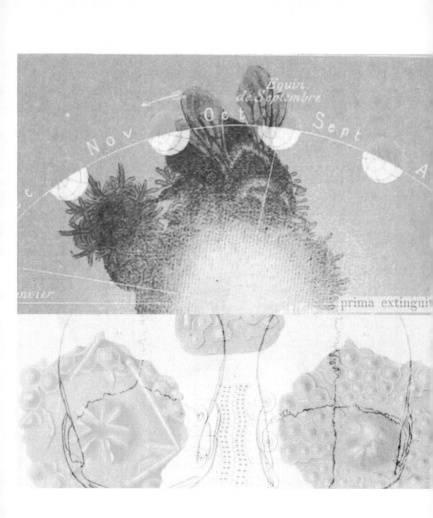

Fig. 6 **Prima Extinguitur**

FROM A PLANE

Across the valley, vacancy: roads unspool,
words undo themselves on the page.
Mountains serrate the prairie's face.

Passing by, their ridges dilate sight's locality,
sputter and shift against the metric of the eye.

Moments ago, you sat at terminal's end,
twiddling your thumbs, ticking out
the intervals you'd lose to a blue screen.

Memory's a thin horizon; so, too, is the sky.
Its depth collects the dawn, the day.
Your feed eats the time away.

ACKNOWLEDGMENTS

Thank you to the editors of the following publications, in which this work first appeared, sometimes in an earlier version:

The Adroit Journal: 'The Provinces'
Berkeley Poetry Review: 'Mountain Song'
Free Verse: 'Gradient'
Hunger Mountain: 'Small Version of a Long Story'
Iterant: 'From a Plane'
Jet Fuel Review: 'Glossolalia'
Mantis: A Journal of Poetry, Criticism, & Translation: 'Scalability' and 'Wintering'
Quarterly West: 'Bolted | Tarred' and 'Sur Les Terrains'

Part three of 'Gradient' was printed as a broadside by Candace Jensen, in celebration of *Deep Green Query*, Jensen's solo exhibition at Brooklyn's Amos Eno Gallery. My deep thanks to Candace for her ongoing collaboration, as well as to Timothy Donnelly and Lynn Xu, who took part in the show's Ecopoetics Salon.

'From a Plane' received the Dorothy Rosenberg Memorial Prize for a lyric poem from the University of California, Berkeley. Thank you to the prize committee and to the Department of English at Berkeley for supporting my work, financially and otherwise.

Gratitude to the small cadre of friends, teachers, and colleagues whose eyes first alighted on this project or parts of it, among them Ann V. DeVilbiss, Jessica Farquhar, Carolyn Forché, Julia Guez, Dave Harrity, Jewel Pereyra, Kristi Maxwell, Kristen Renee Miller, Caleb Perry, Ken L. Walker and Kelly Weber. Thanks, too, to Todd Swift, Amira Ghanim, and Black Spring Publishing Group for making this little book possible. I am indebted to the British Library, whose archives on Flickr Commons sourced much of the visual material collaged here. Special thanks to Simone Muench and Stephanie Karas at *Jet Fuel Review* for nominating 'Glossolalia' for a Pushcart Prize.

Most of these poems were written in Washington, DC, during the early months of 2018. I am grateful to those who sustained me throughout that time, and to those who do so today: Sarah, Clementine, Wendell, Mom, Mike, Shelby, Joe, Izzy, Zooey, and Simone—and to Kimi Jo, willing auditor and close companion, especially throughout the writing of these poems.